"HANDS ACROSS THE WATER"
WINGS TOUR USA

BOOK DESIGN BY HIPGNOSIS
ALL PHOTOGRAPHS BY AUBREY POWELL
GRAPHICS AND ILLUSTRATION BY GEORGE HARDIE
EDITED BY STORM THORGERSON & PETER CHRISTOPHERSON
PHOTOGRAPHIC PRINTING BY BILL ROWLINSON
PRODUCED BY MPL COMMUNICATIONS LIMITED

LONDON

17 MAR

REED BOOKS
Los Angeles
Published in North America by Reed Books
A subsidiary of Addison House, Inc.,
Morgan's Run, Danbury, N.H. 03230
© Copyright 1978 MPL Communications Ltd.

Originally published by
Paper Tiger, A Dragon's World Limited Imprint
Limpsfield and London.

ISBN LIMPBACK 0-89169-500-1
Library of Congress Catalog Number 77-18483.

Printed in Spain by
Printer Industria Grafica S.A.
Sant Vicenç dels Horts 1978
Deposito Legal B-817-1978

Aubrey Powell, or Po, as he is more commonly known in the business, and believe me, he is commonly known, came with us on our 1976 American Tour and during the many concerts we played, managed to get into just about every situation there was to be got into.

As he went he snapped the shots you will find in this book, and later put the whole thing together with his friend and ace graphics man, George Hardie.

Ever since he has been trying to get me to write this introduction, and as usual it is a last minute job.

So, Po, here you go.   Paul McCartney

The pictures in this book are an attempt to present a clear and personal view of what happens on a rock 'n' roll tour. The view is ours and the tour is that of Paul McCartney and Wings across the U.S.A. in May and June '76. It's intended to be a kaleidoscope of places, people and events as opposed to a precise piece of reportage. They are in effect pictures taken on a tour rather than of a tour.

Since we've been on rock 'n' roll tours before, and had an idea of the kind of things that went on, we decided to impose an arbitrary plan. This was to photograph on or very near to the hour: thus the order is relative only to the hour of the day rather than to the narrative or geographical sequence. Take an hour like 8 am, and one can find that someone on tour may be in bed, someone else may be arranging the equipment, and someone else still may be doing some sort of vigorous exercise. It was then a simple decision to be in a few different places at different hours.

Pictures were selected both for individual quality or for their information value – for how they refer to the overall mood and also how they describe specific things or places. For example, much of the tour consists of moving from one box into another box: the band go from limousine to hotel room, back to limousine, then into dressing room, back again into limousine to go to hotel room to get back into limousine in order to board the aeroplane. So we show an empty hotel room or dressing room. On the other hand we also include pictures like the drifters of Chinatown, usually for their own sake, but remembering that although it was only fleetingly glimpsed, it was a town that the tour visited, and stayed maybe a day. And we looked too for any pictures that might do both, like the shot of musicians tuning up, or some of the audience affirming their delight.

Contrary to some opinion, tours represent a lot of hard work and in spite of spasms of alarming unreality that may occur, it is basically a very real and grinding operation. We chose therefore to work in black and white rather than in colour. It seemed to us that the last thing that was required would be to make it more glamourous than it was.

Tours in general and this tour in particular oscillate – it's fantastic and repetitive by turns; it's play and work; it's moving and dynamic, and then it's sluggish and meandering. It can be a long and massive operation involving a large cast of musicians, organisers, roadies, drivers and vehicles. Maybe this tour had an extra dimension since it was hailed as the return of a prodigal. Either way it's often a question of endurance, of just starting out at the beginning and persevering as well as one can until the end. A rock 'n' roll tour is an event, best seen perhaps in its entirety and not merely as a jumble of dislocated highlights.

That's what this book is about.   Storm Thorgerson

LONDON

30 JULY

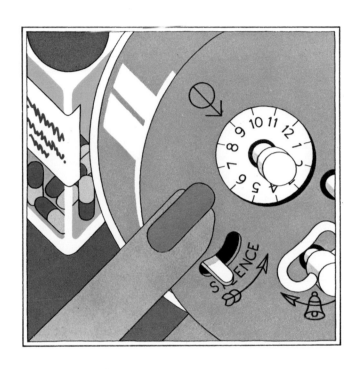

Paul and Linda McCartney's house

DALLAS

2
MAY

SEATTLE
10 JUN

Joe English

LOS ANGELES

21 JUN

Brian Brolly (Manager) and Geoff Ardent (Bodyguard)

DALLAS

1
MAY

Jack Maxson (P.A. Sound Mixer) and Morris Lyda (Monitor sound mixer)

John Hammel (Road Manager) and Trevor Jones (Road Manager)

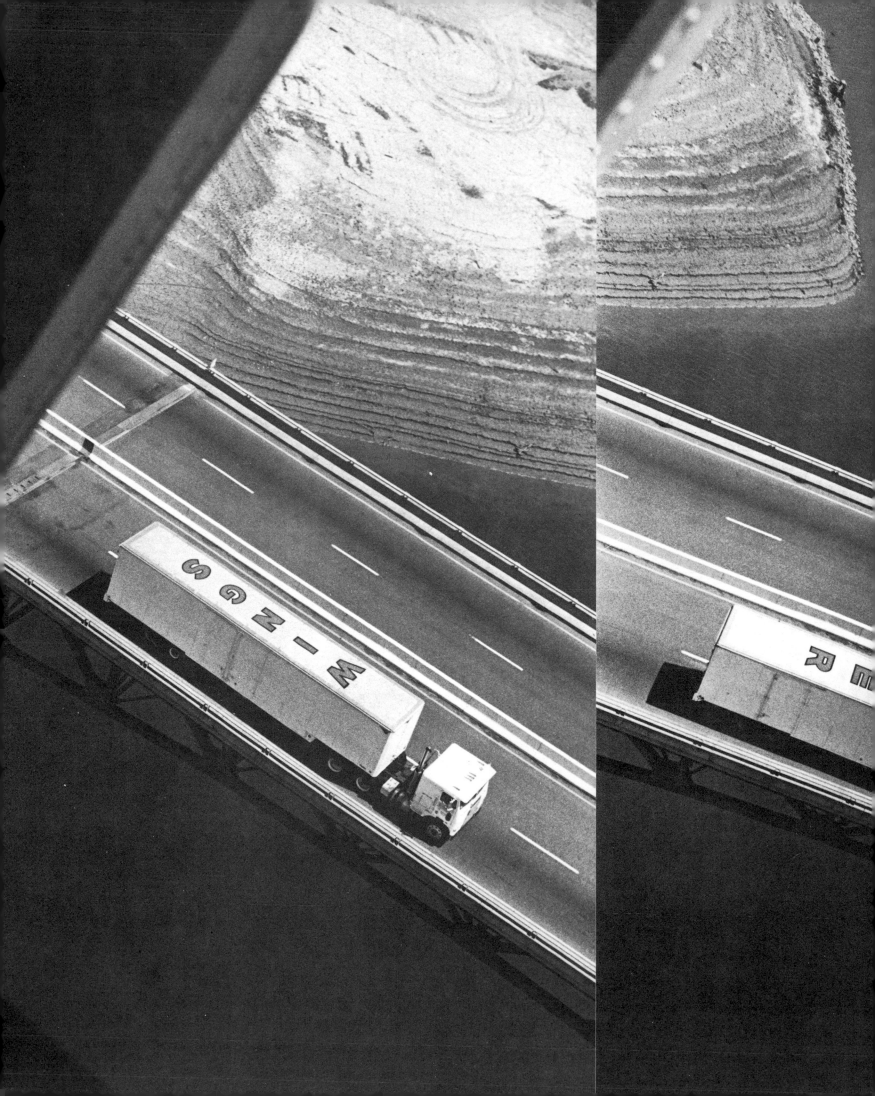

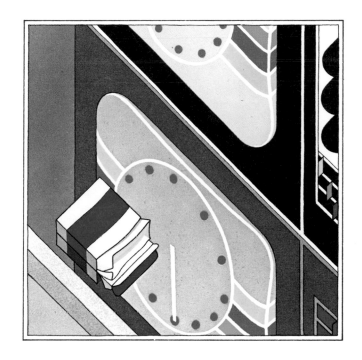

CHICAGO   NEW YORK   ATLANTA

2 JUN   **23** MAY   **19** MAY

Orrin Bartlett (Director of Security)

Jimmy McCulloch

Chinatown

NEW YORK

17
MAY

Frank Lloyd Wright buildings

Century City   Haight-Ashbury

LOS ANGELES

19
JUN

SAN FRANCISCO

14
JUN

Golden Gate Bridge

La Salle Building

Madison Square Garden

NEW YORK

24
MAY

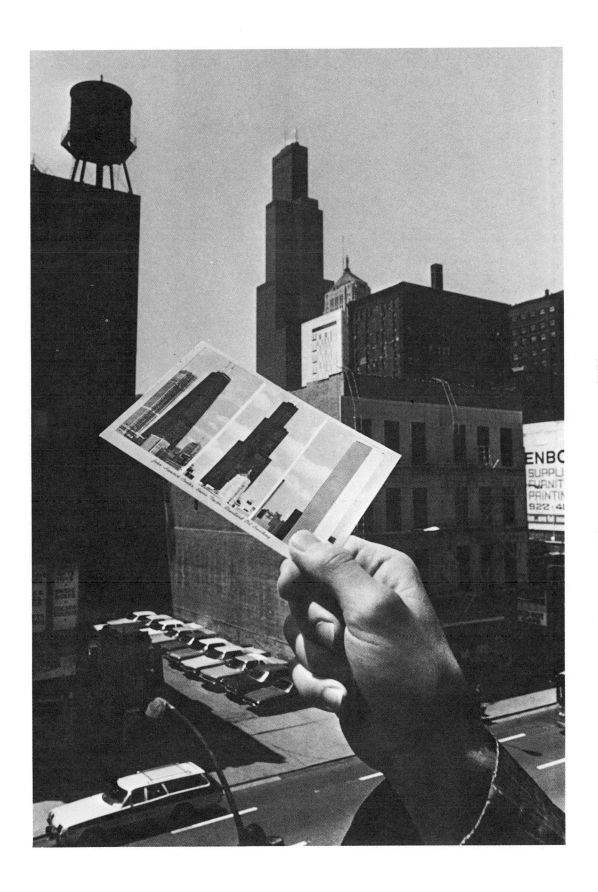

Sears Tower

CHICAGO

2 JUN

J. F. Kennedy Memorial

Site of the Kennedy Assasination

Crew of Wings' private plane

NEW YORK

11
MAY

Morton West (Director of limousine services)

Hotel bar

LOS ANGELES

7
JUN

Wings

NEW YORK

22 MAY

Paul McCartney

Denny Laine

NEW YORK

18 MAY

Wings before take-off

NEW YORK

22 MAY

Wings before take-off

Linda McCartney and Brian Brolly in flight

Paul McCartney and Howie Casey in flight

IN FLIGHT

22 MAY

Denny Laine

Mr. and Mrs. Tony Dorsey

King Dome

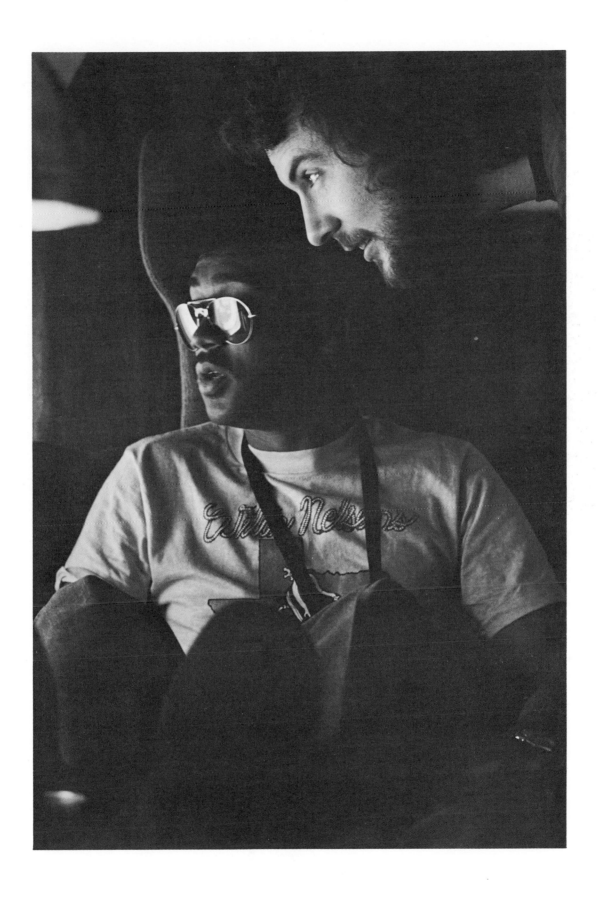

Thaddeus Richard and Steve Howard

TUCSON

18 JUN

Police escort. Limousine drivers

WASHINGTON

15
MAY

Musical reception

BOSTON

22 MAY

Jimmy McCulloch, Joanne and Denny Laine   Roadside

LOS ANGELES
21
JUN

DETROIT
7
MAY

Off-duty policeman

CHICAGO

2 JUN

Paul and Linda McCartney's house

LOS ANGELES

22
JUN

Family portrait

Family portrait

NEW YORK

24
MAY

Family portrait

ATLANTA

18
MAY

Main Street

Tour cameraman and sound recordist

Paul and Linda McCartney's children and housekeeper at rehearsal

Showco directors Jack Maxson, Jack Calmes and Rusty Brutsche

Showco's Ian Knight (Stage Designer) and Ted Tittle (Lights)

Riggers

Riggers

CINCINNATI

27 MAY

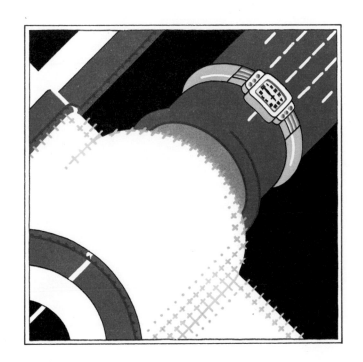

Denny Laine

CHICAGO

3 JUN

Paul McCartney

Linda McCartney

Steve Howard and watchtower

ATLANTA

18
MAY

Waiting for the gig

BOSTON

22
MAY

NASSAU · LONG ISLAND

21
MAY

Police outrider

Arriving for the gig

Waiting for the gig

SAN FRANCISCO

13 JUN

Waiting for the gig

LOS ANGELES

13
JUN

Police briefing

FORT WORTH

3 MAY

Gig security

Gig security

CLEVELAND

10
MAY

Gig security

Richfield Coliseum

CLEVELAND

10
MAY

Paul McCartney's sound check

Horn section sound check

SAN FRANCISCO

13
JUN

Paul McCartney and Jack Maxson sound check

SAN FRANCISCO

14 JUN

Paul McCartney's dressing room

Linda McCartney's dressing room

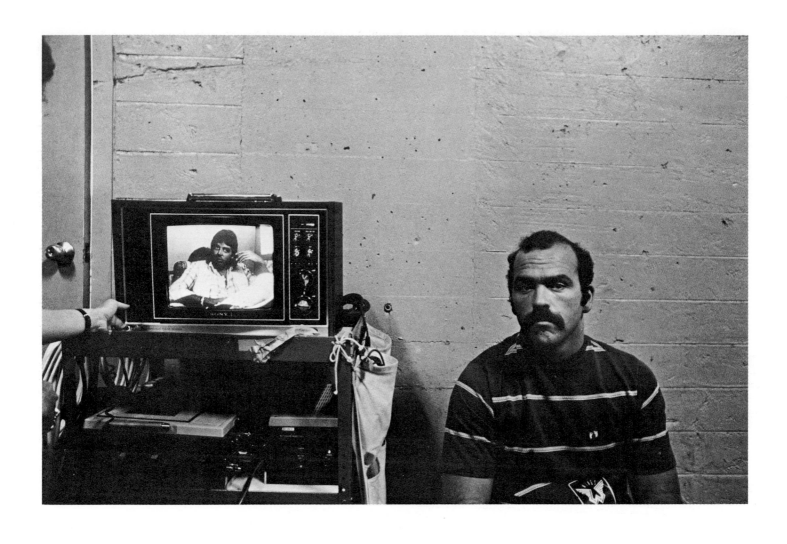

Bodyguard outside dressing room—interview inside

SAN FRANCISCO

13
JUN

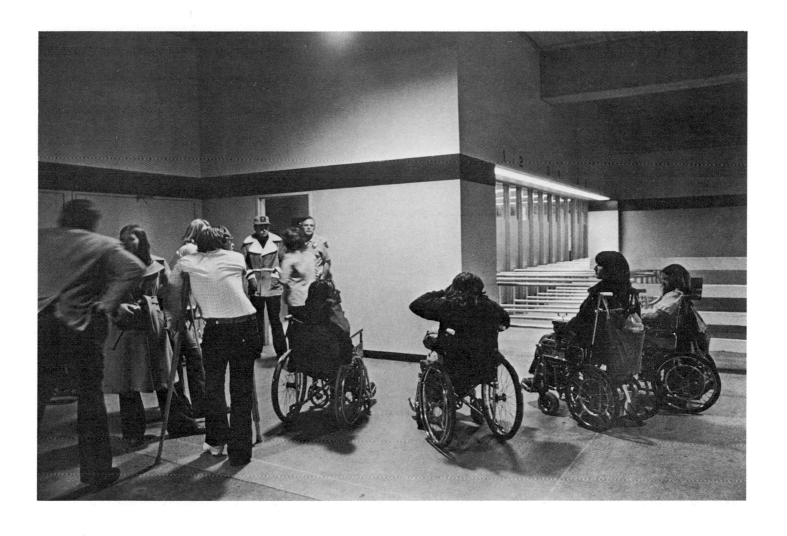

Waiting for the gig

Shirt and picture vendors

BOSTON

22
MAY

Santa Monica pier

ATLANTA

18 MAY

LOS ANGELES

22 JUN

Larry Fitzgerald (tour promotor) and Brian Brolly

CLEVELAND

10 MAY

Lee and John Eastman (Lawyers)

Terry Bassett (Tour promotor)

DALLAS

27
APR

Arthur Wirtz—Owner of Chicago Stadium

CHICAGO

1
JUN

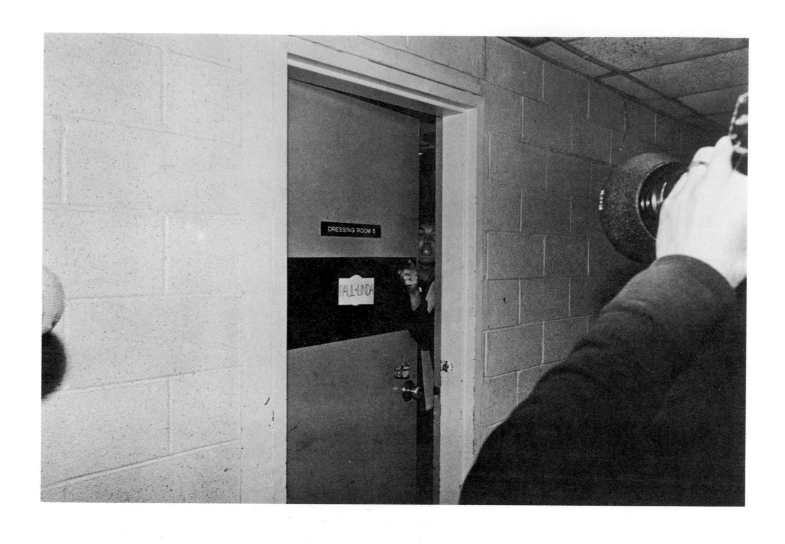

Film crew at dressing room—Madison Square Garden

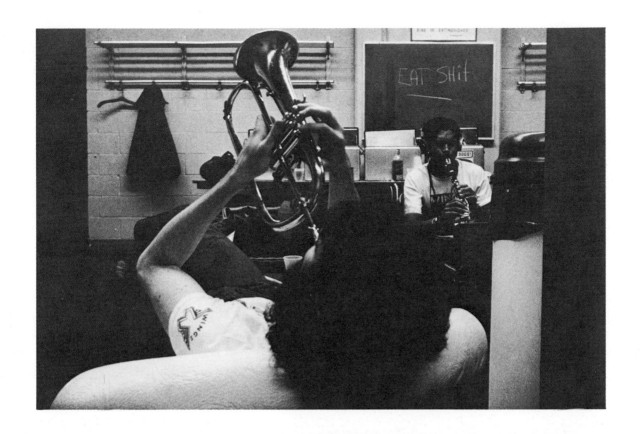

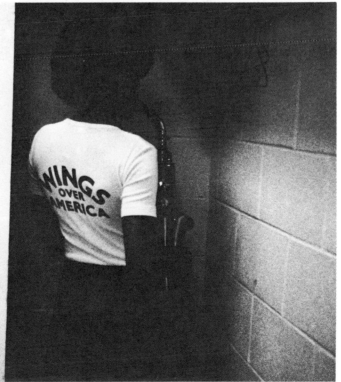

Dressing Rooms

Paul and Linda McCartney

CHICAGO

1 JUN

Allan Williams (Beatles' original manager)

Gig reception

With Roy Harper and Peter Frampton

Elton John and Cher arrive

PHILADELPHIA
14 MAY

LOS ANGELES
21 JUN

Concession people

Concession people

ATLANTA

19
JUN

About to go on—Madison Square Garden

NEW YORK

24 MAY

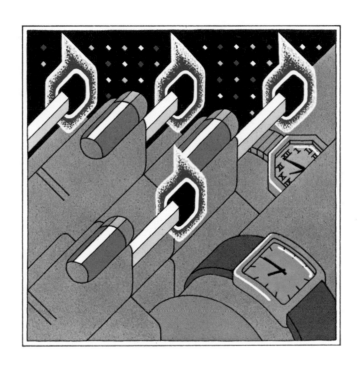

Paul McCartney on stage

Jimmy McCulloch

Linda McCartney

Joe English

Denny Laine

Paul and Linda

Denny Laine

Acoustic sets

Paul sings 'Yesterday'

Joe

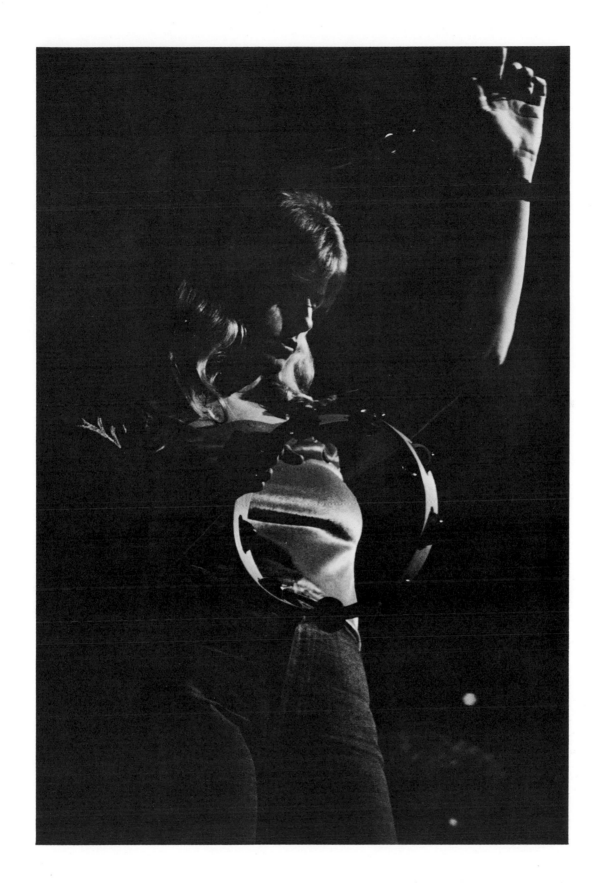

Linda

Jimmy

Denny

Backstage

HOUSTON

4
MAY

Backstage at Madison Square Garden

NEW YORK

24 MAY

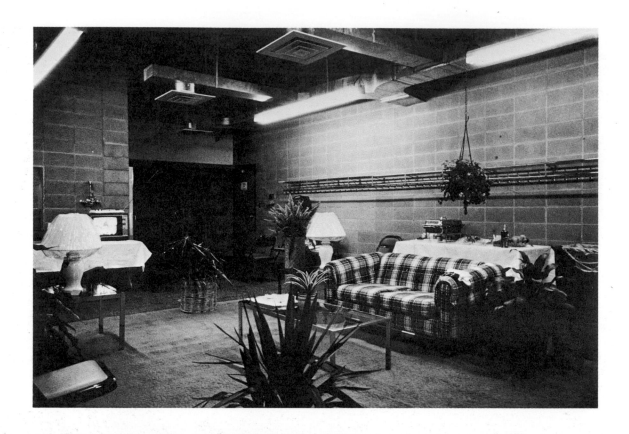

Dressing room before and after

CINCINNATI

27 MAY

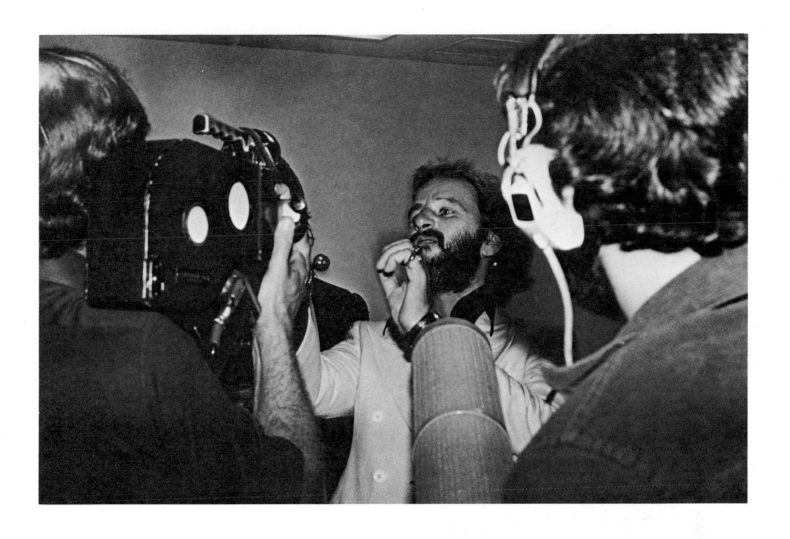

An old friend backstage

LOS ANGELES

21
JUN

Denny Laine with Mother and Father

NEW YORK

25
MAY

Paul McCartney's birthday party

TUCSON

18 JUN

Humphrey Ocean's birthday party

LOS ANGELES

22 JUN

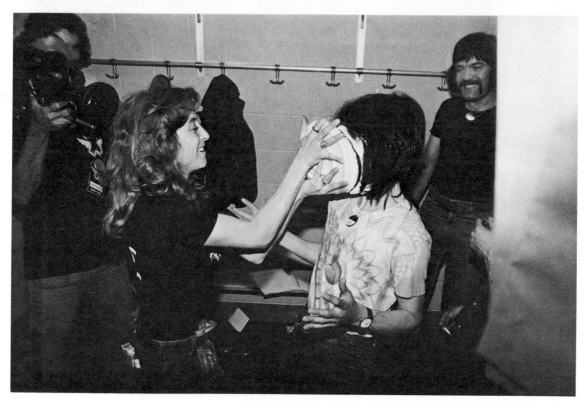

Jimmy McCulloch's birthday party

Madison Square Garden

NEW YORK

24
MAY

Leaving the gig

Wardrobe mistress

CLEVELAND

10 MAY

Tour cameraman

DETROIT

8 MAY

Truck driver

CHICAGO

2 JUN

Security guard at the hotel

Jimmy McCulloch

LOS ANGELES

21
JUN